Live, Laugh and Let Go

Live, Laugh and Let Go

An autobiography

GUL HINDUJA

JAICO PUBLISHING HOUSE

Ahmedabad Bangalore Chennai
Delhi Hyderabad Kolkata Mumbai

Published by Jaico Publishing House
A-2 Jash Chambers, 7-A Sir Phirozshah Mehta Road
Fort, Mumbai - 400 001
jaicopub@jaicobooks.com
www.jaicobooks.com

LIVE, LAUGH AND LET GO
ISBN 978-93-93559-89-0

First Jaico Impression: 2023

Page design and layout by R. Ajith Kumar, Delhi

Printed by
Thomson Press India Limited, New Delhi

For my wife Kanta, who has been my anchor and best friend in the journey of life.

CONTENTS

FOREWORD

"Gul" means rose in Persian, a flower in Urdu and Sindhi. True to his name, Gul Hinduja spreads fragrance with his jolly nature and radiates his inner beauty all around.

I first met Gul sometime in the early 70s when he travelled to Iran for business and I had gone to receive him at the airport. We were based in Tehran since the days of my late father who had established our family business there. But our families went back a long way, to the days in Shikarpur from where our *biradari* (fraternity) hailed, then in undivided India and known as the Venice of the East. It was only customary for us to share our experiences and anecdotes over many lunches and dinners together.

Gul's life has been one of numerous challenges met with fortitude and resoluteness. He often confided in me what he was going through and looked up to me for advice which I was always happy to provide. We both share a love for music and songs. The most distinct memory of Gul in my mind is of him dancing also while singing '*Be-Bop-a-Lula*'. Like me, he too breaks into old Hindi songs to uplift everyone's mood around. That is why he remains one of the key pillars of our friendly group. During Covid lockdowns, it was Gul who suggested and insisted that our close group of friends comprising people from different walks of life–professionals to musicians to business–have biweekly zoom sessions and the practice continues.

An extremely helpful person, Gul is dedicated to the cause of education through the IndusInd Foundation, be it for students or senior citizens. It is because he wants to leave a legacy of his experiences for the younger generation, he is writing this book to share his memoirs.

Gul has always looked upon my elder brother, Srichand*, and me for guidance, and is friendly with our younger brothers, Prakash and Ashok. Together, we Hinduja brothers wish him all success for this book and in his future endeavours.

God bless,
Gopichand P Hinduja
Chairman, Hinduja Group

*Srichand P Hinduja passed away on May 17, 2023.

AUTHOR'S NOTE

In December 2019, I was approaching an important milestone in my life—80 years of a memorable journey in this beautiful world. I casually mentioned it to my family and they gave me the most heartwarming gift—a celebration with everyone who had touched my life directly or even fleetingly, all gathered under one roof. An evening filled with warmth, laughter, emotions and banter, it was a celebration I will always cherish. They gathered mementos, made a film on my life using forgotten photographs, and frankly, left me quite overwhelmed. Everyone was so excited about this event, that they forgot to correct me. I had 'completed' 79 and had stepped into my 80th year. This small mathematical error nudged me to think about the legacy of memories I wanted to leave behind.

I had one whole year to think about how 'I' wanted to commemorate my landmark birthday. My life had been touched by grace. I certainly did not have the brains, skills or acumen to deserve or make the kind of fulfilling life I have led. Some divine power had taken care of me.

I baulked at the idea of a book that was all 'I, Me, Myself'. Is there anything more tiresome to a keen reader? Would the lessons I learned be useful to somebody else? Could they entertain, if not inform, the readers?

So instead of a book singing my praises, here are some short stories about a simpleton's journey through life. I hope they make you laugh, but most importantly, they make you realise what you want from life. The most important lesson I hope you take away from my book is "Don't worry, be happy! Everything happens for the best."

PREFACE

This book is the story of my grandfather's life, told in his own words. As a child, I loved listening to stories about his adventures and experiences. His tales always captivated me and left me wanting to know more. So, when I discovered that he had written an autobiography, I was thrilled.

His autobiography is a testament to his incredible life. From his childhood to his experiences in war, and his eventual migration to a new country, his story is full of triumphs and struggles, joys and sorrows. But it's more than just a chronicle of events; it's also a reflection on what it means to live a good life.

As I read through the book, I was struck by his honesty and vulnerability. He shares his successes and failures, his joys and disappointments, and his hopes and fears. He doesn't shy away from the difficult moments and celebrates the moments of happiness and love that he's experienced.

I hope this book inspires readers and serves as a reminder that no matter what challenges we face, we have the strength to overcome them. And I hope it encourages others to reflect on their own lives and what they want to accomplish.

Pushan Hinduja

ONE

THE BOARDING PASS

As soon as I turned 80, it felt like I had got hold of the boarding pass for my flight to the next destination. This pass is our gateway to enjoying a journey from the moment we get it at the airport. So how can we ever be disappointed when we get a boarding pass in life?

THE JOURNEY TO THE OTHER WORLD IS NOT IN OUR HANDS, BUT WE MUST FOCUS ON ENJOYING THIS LIFE TILL OUR LAST DAY.

Now whenever I look at my watch, I'm reminded of losing precious time to make lasting memories. The journey to the other world is not in our hands, but we must focus on enjoying this life till our last day. This epiphany has made me live my life in fifth gear—to have more fun with my friends, family and loved ones and do the things I am most passionate about.

In the twilight of my life, I have cultivated many rituals. One of them includes an evening habit—a cup of coffee from Kala Ghoda Cafe, in Mumbai's art district, a stone's throw away from my office.

My way of showering attention on the people I love is to get on their nerves. At home, my ritual is to irritate my wife, the staff at home, grandchildren and other people who are a part of my daily life, including my yoga teacher (Chaitali) and office assistant (Priyanka). A good heart cannot be 'bought' at any cost and has to be 'manufactured' by oneself. When Kanta, my wife, serves me pineapple for breakfast, I tell her, "Oh, is it the season for mangoes!" She snaps, "Does that look like a mango to you?", and I chuckle gleefully. When she asks me to order food from outside or get fruits on my way back home, I purchase them in bulk, which often annoys her. But food tastes better when shared with more people, especially those who help us every day. I am so grateful for this army of loved ones with whom I share my day-to-day life. Their presence and shared laughter fuel me to face the day ahead.

FOOD TASTES BETTER WHEN SHARED WITH MORE PEOPLE, ESPECIALLY THOSE WHO HELP US EVERY DAY.

Exercise, socialising, community service and work fill up my daily and weekly calendar with a high dose of silly moments.

My mission in life now is clear—to serve the less privileged and bring joy to everyone.

This world has been my school, and the most important lesson has been, "As you sow, so shall you reap". I have led a conscious life guided by ethics, values, collaborative spirit and cheer.

On Sunday afternoons, I discuss updates with beneficiaries of the charitable organisations I have been a part of (including the one at Ganeshpuri, on the outskirts of Mumbai) over video-conference. As long as I stay connected with people and can hold a safe space for everyone to feel heard and celebrated, I feel like I am prospering.

A trip to Bhutan in 2018 made me lean more towards inner peace—the only path to ultimate happiness. The only country in the world that measures Gross National Happiness showed me how peaceful and ethical life could be if one developed and strengthened one's inner compass. What I observed while travelling across Bhutan filled me with immense joy. There is no need for traffic signals and zebra crossings because people naturally give pedestrians the right of way. There is no honking on the streets or brutal overtaking. There are no instances of theft or scams, nor do people overconsume material things out of greed. This core identity has kept the nation independent and proud.

THE RICH AND WEALTHY ARE OFTEN LIVING IN A WORLD OBSESSED WITH MONEY, FAME, STATUS, LOOKS AND EXTERNAL VALIDATION. THEY ARE HELD CAPTIVE BECAUSE THEY FEAR LOSING WHAT THEY HAVE.

How different things can be when we develop morality! The rich and wealthy are often living in a world obsessed with money, fame, status, looks and external validation. They are held captive because they fear losing what they have.

Slowly, I understood my father's wisdom in distributing his wealth while he was alive. "I don't want my children to wait for my death. I'd rather give them all the money while I am alive," he would say. This philosophy is echoed in the Swedish death cleaning practice. You go through all your belongings and give away or dispose what you do not need so that your loved ones don't need to do it after you pass on. A close friend also follows the same philosophy. The man is worth about several thousand crores and has given away all his assets to his only son. He doesn't even have a driver for himself, drives everywhere, and lives with his son. When people incredulously ask him if he was afraid that his son would mistreat him in his old age, "So what if he does? I have a daughter, sisters…," he would reply, "There are so many people I have helped. Would they sleep peacefully knowing I was homeless?"

I soon spoke to my sons about my will and the legacy I have built. Families need to have these conversations. It strengthens bonds and protects all members during life and after their loved ones have passed away.

Every once in a while, I think about how I want to die. My infatuation with the world has worn off, and I am ready to board should my flight be announced. I am sure I will meet my friends, parents, relatives and ascended souls of saints in the afterlife.

I am looking forward to it.

I WANT PEOPLE TO LAUGH, SING AND HAVE A GOOD TIME, CELEBRATING THE LIFE I HAVE LIVED.

I am an average man. I have done everything I wanted to; no desire has been left unfulfilled. I have tasted success and given back as much as I could. So I would like to go into the afterlife with the Gayatri mantra on my lips or in my ears. I do not want a solemn condolence or sombre prayer meeting after I am gone, either. Instead, I want people to laugh, sing and have a good time, celebrating the life I have lived.

I often think about the joy radiated by the Nigerian women I saw during one of my work trips. They spoke animatedly, laughed vivaciously and hugged their friends affectionately while catching up. That's the joy I want people who gather to remember me to feel.

As you read the chapters, I hope my journey inspires you to do good, be humble, stay silly, laugh more, ask for help, be confident and trust the process. Because, please remember, it all works out in the end. As the saying goes, "Hari iccha, ya hari kripa".

TWO

IGNORANCE IS BLISS

There is beauty in not knowing and going with the flow.

Youth is a time of development when one cherishes hope. It includes challenging oneself, as it is a time of building and creating the foundation for the life ahead. It is a time of action—fight for justice, dream, and listen to our hearts and explore the world. It is a time when one trusts both themselves and the world around them.

As a teenager, I dreamt of becoming an industrialist. At that tender age, the power of dreams was all I had as a refugee from Sindh in undivided India, with incomplete education and no exposure to English.

Early in life, I learnt that to create an impact in the world, I needed to harness my potential with a burning desire to rise and grow anchored by education.

But did you know I struggled with my studies? I started losing interest in going to school at an early age. Despite that, I didn't stop dreaming. This opened a new door of opportunity. I experienced a tremendous sense of belonging within my community. I am a product of the Sindhi community's spirit. At the age of eight, I went to a Sindhi kindergarten that did not have any English education as part of the curriculum. Soon, I transitioned to another Sindhi school in Chembur Camp and eventually, moved to Khar where I studied till Class 9 in Kamla High School, run by a Sindhi trust. Very impatient to go to college, I left the school and joined an instant coaching class to gain the exalted status of being 'Matric Pass', that is having passed my matriculation exams. My fascination with instant results in youth was similar to what fans of ready-made tea powder seek today. In the old days, passing the matriculation exam was a bona fide qualification that made one worthy of a job. With the help of coaching class tutors, I became a master of exam-focused, guided studying and got the stamp of 'pass' with 40% marks. It was good enough to go to top colleges in Bombay. Fortunately, all these colleges were owned by Sindhi trusts–Jai Hind, KC, National… I did well and got admitted to Jai Hind College under Sindhi quota, but not good enough to pass in the first year of college due to lack of fluency in English.

MY FASCINATION WITH INSTANT RESULTS IN YOUTH WAS SIMILAR TO WHAT FANS OF READY-MADE TEA POWDER SEEK TODAY.

I was ambitious about life and wanted to establish good relations with people from a young age. The values my parents taught me and wisdom gained from every success and failure in my youth have helped me build a stable foundation for this life, my legacy. Despite weathering highs and lows, I have lived with a smile on my face and still believe in the good in this world. I invite you on a journey of letting go, laughing and looking at life with a fresh, light-hearted perspective with my story. Go with the flow, my young friends, and don't worry; treat every life experience as momentary. Nothing is permanent. When we go with the flow, life creates space for new, beautiful directions that lead to a fulfilling life.

My family had moved to Bombay during the Partition. Tulsidas Hinduja, my father, had swiftly conjured up a finance brokering practice and moved the seven family members from a 12x15ft room in Barrack no T46, Chembur Camp, to a two-room flat in Khar. My brothers Balram and Shyamlal accelerated the family's fortunes with their blossoming businesses. Since our mother expired after the partition, Balram shouldered all the day to day responsibilities along with working closely with my father to build a flourishing business. Balram was educated, broad minded, kind, and very liberal with each of the siblings within the family. Shyamlal wasn't sufficiently qualified to do any work but assisted my father.

Initially I enjoyed the comforts that came with belonging to a well-to-do family, rubbing elbows with the rich, famous and influential in the city. However, it soon dawned on me that I was beginning to take my life for granted. My academic progress was waning and I was moving in reverse gear.

I was struggling with the idea of studying engineering when I was at Jai Hind College. The more I thought about what I wanted to do in life, the more I resonated with a voice within me, which said, "Why be a servant when you can be the master? Become an industrialist and employ dozens of engineers." I just had to find out how the manufacturing business works and set up some factories. I convinced my father that I had finally found something better than repeating a year in college—study abroad.

With my father's guidance, I requested one of his clients to get me an apprenticeship with his business. He imported ball bearings from the biggest manufacturer in Germany. I bagged the chance to start a new chapter of life with dreamy eyes on a hardworking note in new, greener pastures outside India.

My friends were livid with envy. Here they were, still struggling in school, while I—the good-for-nothing ninth-standard-fail—had not only spent a year in college but was also going abroad!

But I was about to learn that things are not as they seem. Great victories can turn out to be rich cloaks hiding failures, and grave failures could be seeds of unimaginable success.

Instead of heading straight to Germany, I was advised to stop in London, as the job training in Germany needed preparation and organisation before I reached.

At the airport, it seemed to me that everyone we knew came to see me off. I chose to fly Air India because I only spoke Hindi and Sindhi, and the prospect of responding to a stewardess' accented English was daunting. As the plane took off, the gravity of my decision dawned on me. I had left behind everything I knew for an unfamiliar, cold continent. It was an emotional moment that I hadn't experienced ever before.

GREAT VICTORIES CAN TURN OUT TO BE RICH CLOAKS HIDING FAILURES, AND GRAVE FAILURES COULD BE SEEDS OF UNIMAGINABLE SUCCESS.

But there was kindness waiting for me, right at the next seat.

Seated next to me was a Gujarati man with a pharmaceutical business. As we started chatting, he realised that where I was scheduled to stay was quite far from London. He firmly said, "You can't go there after we land. You'll have to stay overnight at a hotel."

The sixth of seven children, I was not used to thinking

about survival. My elder siblings and parents had always taken care of everything. Now suddenly I would have to find a hotel in a foreign country—and I didn't even speak English.

But as always, lady luck was my companion and friend. "I have a room booked in Regent Palace Hotel at Piccadilly," my new friend told me. "You can stay with me for one night."

THE GRAVEST REALISATION WAS THAT I LACKED THE TOOLS TO MAKE MY WAY FORWARD IN LIFE—NO SKILLS, QUALIFICATIONS OR JOB PROSPECTS.

In the 24 hours that followed, I got my first taste of European life.

Each day I waited for news about my employment in Germany, the dream drifted further away. On my trunk calls from India, Mr. Chatterjee, whose company I was to work for, would reassure me that I would get the job soon but could never say when.

When stuck in England, let's become an Englishman, I thought and soon enrolled in English-speaking classes.

After a few months, it hit me that I would not go to Germany, and this epiphany filled me with shame. I thought of how much of my father's money I had wasted and the ridicule that awaited me back home. The gravest realisation was that I lacked the tools to make my way forward in life—no skills, qualifications or job prospects.

As I wandered through the wet, grey streets of London, a sign proclaimed a trade fair for automobile industry manufacturers. This piqued my interest since it was a booming sector in India and my family already had a foot in the door. The dream of becoming an industrialist flickered alive again.

I put on my only formal suit and went to the fair.

"You want to open a factory in India?" I asked at every counter, my English still not very sound. Finally, undaunted by refusal, I struck gold with a company called Transport Brakes Ltd. based in Bath Road, Bristol, UK. "Yeah, okay," said the firm's representative. I explained my family's background, and together we crafted an agreement that would help me set up a factory to manufacture brake lining and discs in Bombay.

I sat on the plane back home with the agreement on my lap. I felt like a triumphant hero.

Being ignorant helps one stay humble and blissful no matter what situation life throws at you.

The insolent teenager who went to London was a different man when he returned. In my head, I was already an industrialist and carried myself with that gravitas—gone were the days of indulgent and raucous jam sessions at Volga, or dancing to a live band at Napoli and Berry's. No more marathon drinking sessions or rounds of billiards at the National Sports Club of India. I even stopped frequenting the semi-nude cabaret at the Blue Nile in Churchgate. I took to speaking in monosyllables and wore formal clothes all the time. My demeanour declared that I had no interest in childish frivolities.

GONE WERE THE DAYS OF INDULGENT AND RAUCOUS JAM SESSIONS AT VOLGA, OR DANCING TO A LIVE BAND AT NAPOLI AND BERRY'S.

Once I returned to India, I set up a meeting with the Director General of Technical Development (DGTD) of the country's technical permits department in Delhi. I had been advised, "He will clear the sanctions necessary for you to set up a manufacturing unit."

In Delhi, the DGTD representative looked at my documents. "Hmm…," he said mysteriously. "This would be classified as a foreign enterprise since the parent company is British. So we can't permit this."

The Indian economy liberalised only in the late 90s. In the early 1960s, the government's intentions focused on helping homegrown industries, and the tangled bureaucracy left behind by the British shackled all endeavours. The few industrialists who had muscled, bulldozed, bribed, cajoled, married and fed their way into the system were determined to keep others out. The whole pool was small and petty, and the only way to get a foot in the door was through a tout who knew how to grease the wheels of this mammoth machinery.

All my dreams came crashing down. I had already bought 5,000 square metres of land in Powai for Rs 1, 25, 000 with my father's help. *This is where I will set up my factory*, I had thought. And now, the government official had smashed my dreams. I was, after all, just 22 years old and had never really worked in my life. A slightly more seasoned business person would have recognised the official's denial as a ruse to extract a big favour and found a way in. My father was just a finance broker, not an industrialist.

THE FEW INDUSTRIALISTS WHO HAD MUSCLED, BULLDOZED, BRIBED, CAJOLED, MARRIED AND FED THEIR WAY INTO THE SYSTEM WERE DETERMINED TO KEEP OTHERS OUT.

Inexperienced and naïve, I was left with a piece of paper worth nothing and a large plot of land in the middle of nowhere. So, with my brother's advice and a broken heart, I sold the Powai land but managed to make a profit out of it.

My desires gave me the drive, and my ignorance helped me be humble and blissful, which helped me gain so much knowledge along the way. I was no longer interested in being the most intelligent person in a room or the most successful. Instead, I embraced my ignorance so that people would help me grow with their guidance and mentorship.

Quietly, with the blessing of my father and brothers, I set up several thriving small and medium businesses over the next few years. My nuts-and-bolts factory in Saki Naka, Andheri, Bombay heralded the good times. I had started the factory in partnership with a mechanical engineer, Roopkumar Ajwani, and the finished goods were exported to many countries in east and central Africa, and the Arabian Peninsula. However, as I travelled to these regions, I realised that my factory could satiate only about 10 per cent of their demand for nuts and bolts. So I expanded my business by becoming a dealer; I would procure nuts and bolts from other manufacturers to create a supply chain to fulfil demands from these countries.

The business growth improved our financial situation, and along with my wife and two young sons, we moved to a new flat in Cuffe Parade, Bombay's affluent neighbourhood. I bought the flat in 1970 and in three years, paid the entire amount to the builder to take possession of our new abode.

But the night we shifted, I was informed of a unique situation waiting for me. Bankruptcy.

Don't go to a business, field or profession you don't know much about on someone's advice.

Just as things were going well, another engineer acquaintance, Mudhani, nudged me to dream bigger. "You already have a well-lubricated distribution network across Africa and Arabia," he said, "Why don't you get into the pipe-fitting game too?" But my partner Ajwani was not on board. He was a cautious player and didn't want to risk going into a business he knew nothing about, especially since we were doing so well. So he took a share of the profits and bowed out of the business.

I powered up and reached Iraq and set up a meeting with the chairman of the State Trading Corporation of Iraq. The chairman was tall, fair, with the aura of a military man, having completed his compulsory service in the army. When I told him about the plans for my new business, he was thrilled and offered to buy the pipe fittings through a huge tender. I felt like my dreams were coming true. I then went to my friend, who headed a large bank export credit finance department in Bombay, and he readily extended a line of credit to fulfil my export order.

With a spring in my step, I went to Ludhiana, Jalandhar and Amritsar—the hubs of small-scale industries and brought on board many manufacturers to supply pipe fittings for Iraq. With each instalment worth around Rs 20 lakh, I was in the major league now. Mudhani's job was the technical inspection of the consignment before being shipped off to Iraq. However, the first instalment itself exposed the cracks in the shipment of pipe fittings. There were such complaints about the consignment—which had travelled from Punjab to Bombay, and from Bombay to Basra over three months—that the retailers in Iraq refused to accept it. They found the product to be so substandard that all other orders stood cancelled.

MY TITANIC HAD BEGUN TO SINK JUST AS QUICKLY AS IT HAD SAILED, AND MY NEW MANAGER, THE ENGINEER, WAS THE FIRST TO JUMP OFF THE SHIP AND DISAPPEAR.

My Titanic had begun to sink just as quickly as it had sailed, and my new manager, the engineer, was the first to jump off the ship and disappear. "Just because you are my friend," said my Iraqi buyer friend, with a calm presence, "you will not be penalised for your mistakes. But you will have to take back the faulty consignment, and we will not accept any new ones–not the ones on their way to Iraq or those manufactured in Punjab."

Struck by the magnitude of my losses, I returned to Bombay only to find my banker friend waiting for me. Our families had holidayed together in London and Paris recently, and because of this affection, he took a kinder approach. Over an elaborate tea service in my office, he told me that I had only five to six lakh rupees in the bank, hardly enough to pay back Rs 25 lakh that I had borrowed as capital for my venture. The only way out was to file for bankruptcy to throw the bank off my back.

I was not ready to do this. "Bankruptcy will be a public declaration of failure," I replied. "No one will ever do business with me again. No one will trust me with their money. It will sound the death knell for my reputation."

"Do you plan on fleeing the country?" asked the banker calmly as he poured me some tea from a silver teapot. "No!" I cried.

"Will you pay back the bank?"

"Of course!" I said emphatically. "Okay, do you have anything the bank can hold as collateral? Any property?" he asked. Reluctantly, I turned over the papers for my new home in Cuffe Parade and the papers for the factory in Saki Naka.

The banker scanned them lightly with a glance and put them away. Only later did I realise what an act of faith this was—I didn't sign any papers, so I was not legally bound to give up my assets. My friend had just taken my word for it.

Drowning in debt, I could no longer even run my nuts and bolts factory. So I locked it up before my creditors landed there, demanding to be paid. I decided to try to rebuild my luck abroad, with the responsibility of two families depending on me to earn a living—mine and my sister's.

THREE

SUCCESS STARTS WITH EMBRACING FAILURES

After bankruptcy, it felt like my whole world came crashing down. I knew I had to stay focused, present and calm, so I decided to explore a new business opportunity in the Middle East. I explored options in Kuwait and then moved to Jeddah and Dammam in Saudi Arabia but didn't find much luck at work or a sense of community to anchor there. While that exposure opened my worldview to multicultural work environments, I struggled to relate to some of their rigid and ostentatious ways of living.

Finally, I met Mohammed Al Aai, an old customer whom I supplied goods on credit in Riyadh. I reconnected with him on this long road to earn back my lost fortune. I shared my circumstances, and Mohammed listened to me patiently.

Mohammed ran a hardware store and took me to the open storage yard behind his shop with a white hoarding named 'Ba A'bad Hardware' emblazoned in red. "If one business fails, just pick a new name and start afresh," he told me and further cheered me on by saying, "Dream again."

Riyadh is a tough city to live in but Mohammed helped me with 1000 riyals per week and supported me with this loan for 44 weeks to live in the city. It paid the rent for the room I shared with 10 Afghani daily wage labourers in the most crowded lanes of Batha, and helped me buy two shawarmas (wraps) a day, which made my stomach full. How can I ever forget those days?

WITH THE OIL BOOM FUELLING THE REGION'S ECONOMY, BUILDINGS AND HOMES WERE BEING CONSTRUCTED OVERNIGHT. THEY NEEDED HARDWARE ESSENTIALS I COULD IMPORT FROM MY CONTACTS IN INDIA. AND SO BEGAN THE JOURNEY OF REBUILDING MY WEALTH.

Every day, I put on good clothes and set out to find leads for my business. At each hardware store, I stopped to make small talk and ask whether they were falling short of anything. I had a small list of items—tiles, metal fencing, bolts, pipes, pipe fittings and nails. With the oil boom fuelling the region's economy, buildings and homes were being constructed overnight. They needed hardware essentials I could import from my contacts in India.

And so began the journey of rebuilding my wealth. Each day, I would put on the same suit and walk three to four kilometres in the glaring desert sun to glean what was required in the market and then contact small-scale industries in India to supply it. To add to my travails, I was still on a tourist visa and would have to leave Saudi Arabia every month and go to neighbouring Iran to get a new one.

One day, I was sharing my hardships with Hamad, another friend who owned a tile shop in the same market. He considered himself more sophisticated than other Arab traders because he had lived in France and spoke French fluently. "Why are you crying, Sheikh?" he asked me affectionately. "Do you need money?"

"Oh no, I am making enough money now," I said, "But it's a pain to fly out of Saudi every month for my visa. I wish I could get a permanent one, but I will need a sponsor..."

"That's all?" said Hamad, "I'll get you a visa. My shop is also not doing well, so we'll struggle together." Then, tearing off the margins of a newspaper, he suggested we draw up a partnership contract. Since I was responsible for leading all the rough work and liaising needed, I took on a 75% share, while Hamad took on a 25% share for just being the sponsor. Hamad showed this to his more shrewd brother, who told him to reverse it. "As you are the Saudi national," he said, "Gul needs you more than you need him. So you should get more share of the profits."

I refused to get into such a lopsided arrangement, and we finally agreed to be equal partners. With this, Hamad gave me a labourer's visa. It was just a tiny piece of paper, but it ironed out so many of my daily worries.

I continued to work hard every day, believing that money would surely follow. I was able to support my family back in Bombay. The months and years that followed hollowed my cheeks and burned my skin to a crisp. On one trip to India, my wife came to pick me up from the airport in a Fiat with curtains on the windows. As I sat in the driver's seat to take them back, people mistook me for a new driver. *Oh well,* I thought, *this is an experience too.*

I CONTINUED TO WORK HARD EVERY DAY, BELIEVING THAT MONEY WOULD SURELY FOLLOW. I WAS ABLE TO SUPPORT MY FAMILY BACK IN BOMBAY. THE MONTHS AND YEARS THAT FOLLOWED HOLLOWED MY CHEEKS AND BURNED MY SKIN TO A CRISP.

In my endeavour to do better, I cultivated a relationship with Mr Abdul Latif, a defence contractor attached to the Saudi government. Abdul's task was to get whatever the government needed and he would turn to me for fulfilling those requirements. Once, they needed miles and miles of chain-link fencing to cordon and mark a large swathe of government land. I sourced it in India and got it shipped from Bombay. The whole deal could have raised my bank balance by one lakh riyals.

But Abdul Latif was not as prompt with payments as he was with demands. For three to four months, I walked to Abdul's office several times a week, hoping to get paid. But Abdul would make small talk, offer me tea and dates and then come up with an excuse not to pay me that day. When I would get angry and draw Abdul's attention to my troubles, saying I walked daily to his office, Abdul even offered me his old used car, but never actually gave it to me. It dawned on me that though the Arabs relied on Indians to build their nation, they never understood our suffering or saw us as humans.

Finally, one day, Abdul said the government needed a few kilometres of underground cable. I was the only man who could procure it. "But I'll need my commission. I am borrowing money from friends and living for the earlier orders first," I said, seizing the opportunity. "They don't trust us because the payment for the chain-link fencing is still pending. This is sullying the reputation of the Saudi contractors."

"Oh, you have not been paid yet?" said Abdul, feigning ignorance, "Why didn't you say so? Your money is lying right here, you silly man." He pulled out a bundle and counted out the money he owed me.

Every rich man lies to delay, save and swallow a less wealthier man's money.

Thrilled with this jackpot, I first went to my friend Mohammed. I was still living on the weekly allowance he gave me, and with great satisfaction, I flicked 44,000 Riyals in vivid, crisp notes and handed them to my benefactor. "How, who, what… what is this?" stammered Mohammed, befuddled. "It's your money," I said. "One thousand for 44 weeks!"

"Where did you get it from?" he asked.

"I struck a large business deal for chain-link fencing for the government contractors," I shared. Then, it slowly dawned on me that Mohammed was not happy to have his money back.

Mohammed reluctantly took the money but could not bring himself to smile in gratitude, congratulate me, or even offer me the customary bottle of mineral water.

How odd, I thought as I walked home, my pockets weighed down by my newly earned fortune. For the rest of my life, I wondered why Mohammad was not happy with the loan repayment—was it because he would miss his weekly chats with me? Was it because he enjoyed being a benefactor and not an equal? Or was it jealousy?

Whatever it was, I could feel my luck turning around. I spent a few sleepless nights, the rest of the money stuffed into my pillowcase. I was afraid my roommates would beat me and grab it if they found out about the large amount. After sending some money home to my wife, I walked around Riyadh's 60th Street, an affluent neighbourhood dotted with newly built plush mansions with Roman pillars and spacious garages used by owner's drivers. I noticed a 'To Let' signage on the outhouse of one such garage.

AT EACH STEP, A FRIEND WAS WAITING WITH A CONNECTION TO BE MADE THAT WOULD TAKE ME A STEP HIGHER.

It turned out to be a tiny home: Just two rooms, a kitchen and a bathroom on a completely bare stage. The walls were devoid of paint and the floors of tiles. *But,* I thought, *it's in a prestigious area and will be good for my profile.* So I went in and made the down payment with the money I was left with. I finally had an actual home. Hamad, my Francophile friend, gave me the tiles for flooring, and as I took on more construction contracts, I turned the house into a home, bit by bit.

In the years that followed, I was able to become a 'small king' again, as Muhammad had christened me. At each step, a friend was waiting with a connection to be made that would take me a step higher. One friend, for instance, told me casually while I was in Bombay that he supplied labourers to the Gulf. Though I did not see the need for it then, I filed that information away to use later.

Serendipitously, Abdul Aziz, Hamad's friend, once mentioned that though Saudi now had tall commercial buildings, it had not occurred to the buildings' administration to clean them! There was a gap in the housekeeping business and I knew I was just the man to fill it. Abdul assured me that a tender would be floated for the cleaning contract and I would get it if I could get skilled labour to execute the job.

As usual, I accepted the challenge and then went about learning to execute it. I knew that Dallah Avco, a Saudi-American company, was on contract to clean the airport. Nudged by a gut feeling, I went to the airport, bought two chocolates and tucked them into my pocket. It was night and workers were cleaning the premises. As expected, an Indian man was the manager, overseeing the work—a Malayali. "Hello brother," I said and gave him a chocolate. "What's this for?" asked the man. "It's my birthday… I have one for you and one for me."

After eating the treat in companionable silence, I pointed to the rotating floor polisher being used by one of the workers and asked, "What's this?"

"Oh this? This is how we clean the floors."

"Can you teach me how to use it?" I asked.

"Sure. It's effortless; there's nothing to it. The first thing you have to remember is that the machine pulls to the right."

Within a few hours, the man showed me where to pour the liquid soap, how to guide the cleaner across tiled floors and how to maintain it. In turn, I passed this technical knowledge onto about 15 workers my friend had sent from India. I also taught them soft skills—to bow and greet office-goers with a 'good morning' and bid them good night. They were all given gold silk uniforms with the name of my newly-formed company, Alba, embroidered at the back.

Alba was the only company that offered commercial housekeeping and janitor services, and when the government floated the tender, we grabbed it. It was now servicing almost every office complex in Riyadh. I rode the crest of another wave of prosperity. In about three years, when other companies got into the business and the profit margin diminished, I got into the construction contractor business and helped build many grand mansions. At this juncture, my nephew from Indore joined me in Riyadh to assist me with these new plans.

Soon, I moved out of the tiny outhouse on 60th Street and into the modern Olaya residential compound, occupied mostly by expats and affluent Saudis. There I had a huge three-bedroom apartment, a swimming pool and gym, a driver for my cars and a cook from Bombay to rustle up my favourite dishes. The family would visit for the holidays and I got to visit home often.

After about a decade or so in Saudi Arabia, I had amassed enough money to pay back the bank in Bombay. I strode into the bank in Bombay with pride and went to clear all my dues. But much like Mohammad, the new bank manager was not happy at the thought of me being debt-free. The bank dilly-dallied and ho-hummed, saying there was no procedure to clear all of it in one go. "You'll have to pay the penalty," they said.

"Okay, I'll pay it," I said, since I was eager to finally clear my name.

"And then there's the interest on the amount."

"Yes, of course."

"Also, we'll have to charge compound interest on the interest.... At defaulter's rate"

"I understand," I said.

Seeing that there was no way they could keep me indebted to them, the bank reluctantly accepted my money and cleared my dues.

While these negotiations were on, I deposited the money I brought from Saudi Arabia in a new bank account, in US dollars. Ironically, the same manager who gave me the money when I was in crisis headed this new foreign bank where I made the deposit from this new lease of business life.

FOUR

TO HAVE A FRIEND, IS TO BE A FRIEND.

My life in Riyadh blossomed with warmth and friendships. The business flourished and I soon rented a small office in the posh Al Khozama Hotel.

A daily work ritual included my friend, Fatalah Farhand's visit to my new place of work to share his tales of woe and fresh tears. It would invariably involve his benefactor, a princeling in the continental mass of Saudi Arabia's royalty. The prince had been stringing Fatalah for nearly a decade, dangling business opportunities in front of him, making him do menial tasks and never paying him. Every day, Fatalah would come with a new saga of humiliation, and I would send him back with some money for food, cigarettes, entertainment, or to buy affection for a few hours.

During my years in Saudi Arabia, Fatalah had been my close friend. The tall, refined Iranian was the epitome of Persian culture and sophistication. He always dressed sharp, smelled great and spoke in poems and parables. He considered himself a great judge of human character. He was generous to a fault with someone's money. "Give that watch to your driver," he would tell me. And it would be the same way with a shirt or a tie that did not meet his exacting standards or displeased his eyes.

And that was a part of the problem why he was unsuccessful. 'Fattih', as I called him, did not want to make thousands or millions. He had decided to only exert himself for endeavours that would make him a billionaire.

THE RICH ONLY GIVE AWAY WHAT DOESN'T COST THEM ANYTHING.

And that is why he hung around the princeling, lived in a bungalow in the royal compound, driving whichever luxurious car the royal family was not using on that day. When the princeling travelled to Paris or London to get a new set of clothes, he always took Fattih along and bought two of everything–one for himself and one for Fattih. That's the greatest lesson Fattih learned and passed on to me—the rich only give away what doesn't cost them anything.

Fattih was the son of a priest and had studied in Germany. He fell in love and married a German woman and had two children with her. However, competition in the market sunk his means of earning a living—he manufactured fire-fighting equipment. When he landed on the shores of Saudi Arabia, his elegant manners and skill with languages brought him to the royal court. He spoke Arabic, Farsi, English, German and Turkish fluently, and even a smattering of Urdu.

The princeling not only found him efficiently resourceful as a right-hand man who could get anything done but also highly trustworthy and a man of honour. The royal women were as liberal within the compound of the palaces as they were conservative and sheltered outside. Their evenings were indulgent, filled with gambling and alcohol. The men and women descended into disarray as the revelry spiralled into the night. Fattih would politely and respectfully excuse himself to a corner when this happened to save the ladies the blushes in the morning.

This is why the princeling kept him near. Fattih could always be counted on to accompany the numerous royal princesses on their shopping trips to Harrods or Champs-Élysées, and keep a close eye on them as they savoured liberal enchantments of the nightlife in these Western countries.

I always thought I was the better friend and more significant benefactor in our relationship. After all, I was liberal with my money and practically supported Fattih's lifestyle without expecting to be paid back.

But in my twilight years, I realised that Fattih had bestowed me favours I could never repay. They were small gestures, such as holding me back when I was about to act impulsively and out of anger.

After years of an equal partnership with Hamad, my friend and business associate who owned a tile shop, our relationship was beginning to fray. I was doing well in business and would travel to India every month or two to be with my family. When I returned, Hamad would invariably argue with me over it. "Why do you have to go to India so often?" he would complain. "Why not?" I would say. "The business does not suffer. Everything is running smoothly, and I get to see my family at my expense."

Hamad missed someone to talk to, and one day our bickering got so bad that I announced I had enough and ended our partnership. Hamad felt rattled, but his ego didn't allow him to show that. He was a man of great pride, as most Arabs are, so there was no question of him begging me to reconsider my decision. A few days later, he came to meet me and said, "I am concerned about you. You are my friend and still need a sponsor to continue doing business in this country. Here, take my brother Agal."

"I am not very fond of him. He's too outspoken," I shared, frankly.

"Yes, but he's also lazy and won't ask for too much. Give him a fixed monthly sum, and he won't interfere."

Agal was not interested in the construction business that

Hamad and I had built. He was crude and did not treat others with respect. Like many Arabs, he thought other races were beneath him. He was happy with a fixed monthly amount as long as he didn't have to lift a finger. He'd come to the office in Al Khozama to throw his weight around and bark orders that didn't make sense. On one such overbearing visit, he snapped his fingers at me and asked me to vacate the office for him to use for a short while.

"YOU DON'T BITE A DOG IF A DOG BITES, DO YOU?"

I was with Fattih at that time, and as we both left the office, I began ranting to my friend. "That's it, I'm done. Who does he think he is? I don't need him. I'll go back to my country and start some other business."

"Oh my friend, why are you bothered?" said Fattih to soothe me. "If a dog barks, will you respond to him? Will you bark back at him? He's a dog. You are a prince. You don't bite a dog if a dog bites, do you?"

This calmed me, and the next day Agal came back. I could see that he was ashamed of how he had acted the day before because he was extra courteous to me.

Fattih did not just keep me from acting impulsively; he also never refused me a favour. One evening, I asked over the phone, "Hey Fattih, where are you?".

"I'm just coming to see you, my friend," he replied.

"Okay, can you bring two shawarmas (Arabic sandwiches)? I am famished."

Fattih agreed, but it took him a very long time to come—a distance that should have taken just 15 minutes took one hour. "What took you so long?" I asked when Fattih finally arrived.

"Well, I only had the money for two shawarmas, so I walked all the way here," he said.

"What? Are you mad? You should have told me. I would have sent the car to get you."

But Fattih merely shrugged.

In these quiet ways, Fattih had shown me what friendship is and how one can give even when one has no material advantages over others.

Our friendship grew even deeper over the years. When Fattih heard that my wife and I were going to Germany after a holiday in London, he offered that we stay in his house in Heidelberg. He insisted that we visit him in their home. It was a humble one-storey home where his German wife, son and daughter lived. Fattih cooked the best Persian rice dishes, his wife made traditional German potato soup and cheesecakes, and each meal was accompanied by the best wines.

"By when will you be ready for breakfast tomorrow?" Fattih asked Kanta and me as we retired for the night.

"Oh, about 8.30," I said without thinking about it and went to bed.

The following day, I woke up leisurely at 9 am. When I opened the bedroom door to go down to our hosts, I found Fattih waiting there with a tray in hand. In it were croissants, jam, butter, orange juice, coffee and a small flower. "What are you doing here?" I asked, alarmed.

"Waiting with your breakfast, of course," said Fattih "You said 8:30."

"Have you been standing here all this while?"

Again, Fattih merely shrugged.

Travelling to places with different cultures opens our minds to new ideas. For instance, when I visited Fattih in Heidelberg, I felt inspired when I noticed that his wife cleaned the street facing their home every morning. Imagine the change if we all took such responsibility to keep our homes and surrounding environments clean.

This Iranian friend's greatest gift to me was during what could have been my bleakest time, and I did not even realise it until many decades had passed.

I had grown into one of Saudi's most sought-after construction contractors and employed a workforce of about 100 professionals. I built mansions and sky-walled existing commercial structures at the pace of a seasoned chef dicing carrots.

And then, Iraq invaded Kuwait. This development rattled the region with uncertainty about the future.

All business halted. Expats wondered whether they should wrap things up and head home. Fattih and I chatted in my office, lamenting the arduous days ahead. "Why don't you start putting up marble facades on existing structures?" suggested Fattih. "People are not painting their homes anymore, but marble is just lying around." He introduced me to a German engineer, Peter Gutenberg who knew how to lever marble slabs using grooves and notches instead of nails or adhesives. With a German man as the face of the business, I could charge a premium compared to other competing contractors because of the confidence in quality of German technology and experience in my team.

I have experienced two Gulf wars between Iraq and Saudi Arabia and the impact they had on life and business. So when that business petered out, Fattih came up with another idea: "Why don't you refurbish used prefabricated homes and re-sell them? You have the workforce and are paying them to sit around these days. So you could buy them and I'll show you how to refurbish them."

Prefabricated houses could be raised overnight. Each house measured 12 metres by 4 metres, had two rooms, a kitchenette and a bathroom, and was used as temporary shelter by the military or any other enterprise.

ANYTHING WITH THE 'SECOND-HAND' TAG SOLD FAST IN THE COUNTRY, SO I GOT ON BOARD.

I thought it over. Anything with the 'second-hand' tag sold fast in the country, so I got on board. The two of us drove deep into the desert, about 50 kilometres from Riyadh, into an army camp. Fattih took over, spoke to the military man in charge of the camp in Arabic, and sealed the deal. I had just bought 40 used prefabricated homes without seeing them or thinking about how I would get them to Riyadh or where I would keep them. Each of the worn out houses cost 500 riyals.

Those days, before the omnipresence of ATMs, I would carry a few thousand riyals every time I stepped out of home or office. I counted 20,000 riyals in crisp notes, and even as Fattih cautioned me first to think and inspect the homes, I gave them to the person in-charge. Relieved that the houses were my problem now, the army wanted them off its premises as fast as possible.

I needed to quickly find five to ten acres of empty land. Then, finally, Agal came to the rescue. "There's some empty space near my house," he said when I told him of my new problem. "You can put them there." The next day, I hired a crane and a large trailer to bring the houses to the plot near Agal's home. It was adjacent to the highway, which became the biggest boon. My team re-did the windows and floors and hoisted the houses again. This made them visible to anybody passing by.

Before I could put up a board in Arabic declaring, 'Refurbished like New: Prefabricated Houses for Sale', cars lined up to inquire about all this. On the very first day, I sold ten houses for 12,000 riyals each. Then, as more buyers lined up, I increased the house price from 14,000 to 16,000 to 20,000 riyals for each. Once, my greed got so much ahead of me that an Arab client asked, "How can you sell a second-hand house for 40,000 riyals when a brand new one costs the same?"

So I capped the price at a comfortable profit. However, I was still unable to refurbish the houses fast enough to meet the demand. As war loomed, the houses made perfect temporary homes for labourers and other staff.

I got better at selling them. I knew Arabs didn't like an Indian at the helm of a big business like mine, so I'd pretend to be just a manager when someone came to negotiate a new order, especially if they asked for a considerable discount. "How can I give a discount?" I would say, acting helpless. "I work here. I'll ask my boss." If it were someone who was acting very important, I'd pretend to have a conversation on the phone and then say, "We don't usually give discounts, but when my boss found out it's you, he said we'll tell our contractor to give you a discount on transport (sic)."

Kuwait's invasion spiralled into the first Gulf War; the US and its allies got ready to launch Operation Desert Storm. All the buying stopped, and I was stuck with 200 refurbished homes. I would have to leave them to rot and return to Bombay. Just then, a man drove by the plot. He looked around the houses and said he wanted to buy all 200. The man was as big as the famous industrial families like the Tatas and Birlas are in India. He had just secured a contract with the US army to build their base camp.

With the last of the houses gone, I was free—and a millionaire. Agal got a whiff of my success and was consumed with jealousy. He was no longer happy being just a sleeping business partner and demanded a profit cut. Another sponsor, a Lebanese man, took over my camp in

Dammam and refused to pay me for it. Realising these were tough times and the law would not side with me, I packed my businesses and returned to India.

I was in the Gulf for nearly 20 years and life was simple, which helped me save a major part of my earnings and secure my future. As I sat in the plane headed home, I realised one final gracious gesture from my close friend. Fattih had given me the idea for the business, helped me strike the first deal, and taught me how to refurbish the houses. Yet Fattih, the man who lived a simple life, had never demanded a fee or a share of my profits. It was all an act of friendship.

True friends make time for you and are by your side through thick and thin.

Memories of my early twenties when I aspired to be an industrialist.

With my best friend and wife, Kanta, on our honeymoon.

My dynamic father, Tulsidas Hinduja, who moved to Mumbai during the Partition.

With Kanta and my elder son, Sanjay, during one of my early international business trips.

My younger son, Sandeep, greeting his older brother, Sanjay, as he was leaving for his first international solo trip.

Our family of four holidaying in the UK.

With Kanta and Gopichand Hinduja on a family vacation in Canada.

My loving and adorable elder sisters, Savitri (left) and Sushila (right).

With my brother-in-law, Manohar (centre), and elder brother, Shyamlal (right).

Jangoo Motafram, my friend and partner in music and food adventures across Mumbai.

Making memories with close friends P.P. Chhabria (right) and Amar Daulatani (left).

With young students and talented teachers at
Dream Education Centre, Ganeshpuri.

Breakfast at the Juhu House of the Hindujas, celebrating Ashok P Hinduja's
birthday along with SP Hinduja (centre) and friends.

With elder son, Sanjay.

With younger son, Sandeep.

Kanta and me with our doting grandson, Pushan, who has been a big inspiration for me while writing this book.

A family portrait of Kanta and me with our sons, Sanjay (top left), Sandeep (centre) and our grandchildren Kimaya (top right) and Pushan (bottom right).

FIVE

HOW I MET MY BEST FRIEND

The most beautiful chapter of my life was when I met my biggest support system, the anchor through all my Indian and international work pursuits to build this life.

In my UK-return incarnation, I was a tweed suit-wearing gentleman with a stiff upper lip. I focused only on realising my destiny as a young industrialist and was not interested in setting up home and hearth.

My father had three apartments in the city and four cars. But, as with all wealthy and generous men, when Bhau (as he was fondly called) went for walks on Khar Linking Road and Juhu Beach, those who needed favours would trail behind him. Some would present a special seasonal dish or a rare dessert to appease him, while others would introduce a relative who needed a job. Then some brought alliances for his sons, hoping to get into Bhau's good books.

"Look at the photograph. You don't have to meet her" or "Just meet, you don't have to marry her," my father and brothers would say. I was 22 years old, and all the girlfriends I had in college were now married. In the early 1960s, it was uncommon for a woman to remain unmarried after age 20. Soon, I gave in and agreed to meet some women.

Simplicity topped the list of qualities I was looking for in a life partner. "I hope she's not the kind who puts on so much perfume that I can smell it till Khar," I thought as I prepared to meet Shanti Hasija.

WITH WEALTH AND LIFE EXPERIENCE IN MY FAVOUR, I THOUGHT I WOULD HAVE THE UPPER HAND IN THE RELATIONSHIP. LITTLE DID I KNOW THAT SHANTI WAS SUPERIOR TO ME IN EVERY WAY.

Shanti came from a well-to-do middle class family in Peddar Road. Her mother had passed away when she was young; her sister-in-law and elder sisters raised her. When I saw her in a simple pink salwar kameez and no make-up, I thought, *bingo!* I felt a spark when I first saw her that day.

I was looking for a simple, innocent woman to cast in the role of a life partner. Shanti seemed like she would make a good partner to build the foundation of a beautiful life. What I was specifically looking for was someone who had no boyfriends. With wealth and life experience in my favour, I thought I would have the upper hand in the relationship. Little did I know that Shanti was superior to me in every way.

The first time we met, we talked about the usual things–our childhood, hobbies, likes and dislikes. Shanti was soft-spoken and did not strongly oppose anything. She happily accepted whatever life gave her. I was drawn to her purity of heart, and after a few more meetings, we decided to get married.

Shanti became Kanta after marriage, as per Sindhi traditions, and till today, she is the most successful person I know.

As newlyweds, we moved into the apartment I shared with my father in Khar. Knowing the fledgling family still had to find its feet, my father conscientiously gave Kanta and me separate monthly allowances a few days before the new month started.

As a young bride, Kanta took care of Bhau, my father, by making his favourite snacks to pair with his evening drinks. She would help him make his bed later in the night, and in the morning, when he'd sheepishly ask, "I drank too much, no?" she would always reply, "No, no, not at all," to keep his dignity intact. She learned to drive the car and would run errands, do household chores independently and help all family members. That brought her close to my father. During the 17 years after our marriage when my father was alive, Kanta loved cooking for him and was also instrumental in bridging connections and bonds between family members and Bhau.

As we grew more affluent, Kanta, my two sons and I moved into our apartment in Cuffe Parade. But tragedy hit in the form of business failure. So I went to the countries in the Arabian Peninsula, where I had trade relations, to find a way to earn a living.

Kanta was left behind to care for the family and fend off the many small and medium creditors who came knocking at our door every day. In my absence, with her calming presence and my guidance she bravely attended the various court proceedings for the cases filed against me by my creditors that went on for over a decade.

First, we both decided to pull our boys out of their prestigious South Bombay school as we could not afford the fees anymore. To protect them from turmoil and disgrace, we enrolled them into a boarding school in another city. Then, we cut off all other comforts that our lifestyle afforded us and let go of the chauffeurs, several members of the household staff and even sold off some family assets. But Kanta did not complain or become bitter.

After I went to the Gulf, it took me several months to make enough money to send home. I didn't even have the money to make the international call to India, and we could only speak once a fortnight or so. Kanta never asked me for any money. Instead, she ran the house on the money she had squirrelled away for years—money even I didn't know she had. She was smart and wise. She would eat the simplest of foods and ration it to make a rupee go a long way. Just rotis and one subzi, or dal and rice, never both together.

She represented me at all the court proceedings for the cases filed by creditors, drove the car herself and fended off all unsavoury elements who came to our house and the office to ask for money. She held her head high at family functions and community gatherings and worried more about my well-being than hers.

'IF EVERYONE IS HAPPY WITH YOU, THEN YOU HAVE MADE MANY COMPROMISES IN YOUR LIFE. AND IF YOU ARE HAPPY WITH EVERYONE, THEN SURELY YOU HAVE IGNORED MANY FAULTS OF OTHERS.' KANTA IS BOTH!

She loosened the purse strings when she saw that I could rent a home for myself, even if it was the outhouse (driver's quarters) of a bungalow and could buy myself a beat-up car.

As we grew old together, I realised what a pure soul Kanta is. If anyone is disturbed or sad, they call her up—even if they are my friends or from my side of the family. And she is the first to be by someone's side in moments of sadness and joy. She knows that being a compassionate listener can lift a significant load off the sufferer. And she extends this compassion even to those she has met only a few times.

Once, I read somewhere, 'If everyone is happy with you, then you have made many compromises in your life. And if you are happy with everyone, then surely you have ignored many faults of others.' Kanta is both!

In the precious years we have spent creating lasting memories together, I have found Kanta fluent in the language of love. She expresses it in small, daily gestures that seem eccentric, wasteful, or even controlling, but they aren't. And in those expressions, I find myself. We speak the same language of love for each other.

Take for instance, her affection for her niece Bindu, her elder brother's daughter. If I read out a joke or a WhatsApp forward she enjoys, her first instruction is, "Send it to Bindu." When she makes any sweet or culinary treat Bindu wants, she sends a portion of it with the driver. Her family teases her, saying she is exhausting 500 rupees of petrol by sending a chauffeur-driven Mercedes five kilometres away to carry an item worth 50 rupees. "But it's Bindu's favourite," she says.

Fruits are her big passion. They overrun our home—on the dining table, side tables, in the kitchen. So much so that many people think our family is in the fruit business. Every evening, she calls her trusted fruit vendor, asks him what the day's special is, and orders it. First thing in the morning, after she says her prayers, she selects the ripest, perfect fruit and gives it to the cook to chop it up for breakfast for the family. At first, I thought this was controlling. "I can't even eat a banana in my house without my wife's permission," I would grumble. Then, as I grew wise with age, I realised this was like Shabari's act of devotion to Lord Ram. Kanta loves her family so much that she wants to nourish them at the start of their day with only the ripest, sweetest, juiciest fruits.

Unlike me, Kanta does not make fun of others. Where I have 101 specifications for what I want to eat and can be pretty fussy sometimes with food, she never refuses anything anyone offers her.

I have also learnt that while she is clever about saving and managing money, it doesn't hold any value for her. Throughout our lives together, she has been a part of many kitties and always had a few lakhs in cash at home. She willingly gives the money to anyone who asks and forgets all about it. Twice a day, she asks me the value of her stocks in the share market, but it is just information to her; it does not affect her if she loses money.

While outwardly I have lived to irritate my wife, my

respect for her has grown leaps and bounds. I have realised that just like my Iranian friend Fatalah, Kanta stopped me from being impulsive and making the wrong decisions on several occasions. The only difference between them is that Kanta nags.

The most important ingredient of a successful marriage is to be compassionate, put yourself in your spouse's shoes and let go of the baggage.

SIX

A NEW BEGINNING

With 20 years invested in establishing two businesses in Saudi Arabia (one with Hamad in Riyadh and another with Sheikh Abdul Aziz in Al Khobar), the decision to move back to India was not easy. Though financially my business grew and felt stable, emotionally my spirits were dampened. I had been shortchanged by my Lebanese/Saudi partner over a completely built residential camp in Dammam where 1000 contract workers from Egypt, Lebanon, Jordan, Syria, Palestine, India, Bangladesh, Nepal, Pakistan, Thailand, Phillipines and Indonesia lived in second-hand pre-fabricated houses refurbished by my company. It felt terrible to watch my business that had created so much value for the region, come to a standstill. I no longer wanted to rely on Arab sponsors to make a living.

Nothing is permanent in life.

Disheartened, I drove over the King Fahd Causeway to the neighbouring island kingdom of Bahrain and booked into Hotel Intercontinental to think about my troubles. Browsing through my phonebook, I came across the number of an old friend and dialled it.

When the voice on the other end said, "Are you dead, habibi?", I knew my friend, Suleiman Humaid, had missed me. I poured my heart to him while sharing what brought me to Bahrain. "What is the name of your partner," he asked. Suleiman was the CEO of the Saudi government's insurance company, and looked through his rosters and found that my partner, Sheikh Abdul Aziz was a client.

He called up my partner and said firmly, "This is not right. Give Gul his share in the Dammam camp."

"Of course," replied the Sheikh, ashamed that such an influential man had scolded him. He further said,"We've been looking for him to pay him back, but he's not in Saudi..."

Sheikh came to meet me with large gestures of peace—a bottle of champagne and a bunch of long-stem red roses.

"Oh habibi!" he cried out while striding into the hotel in Bahrain. "Why did you trouble such a big man? We were not going to cheat you…. Come, take this money and let's start a new business together…." But I had learnt an important lesson, "once bitten, twice shy" as a dear friend and advisor would often remind me.

I received my dues from him and with the last rays of hope to explore new business opportunities in the Middle East, I went to Dubai. But I soon realised my heart was not in it anymore and I decided to come back to India. It was the early 90s, and my sons were now grown up men. I had made enough money and wanted to establish a new line of business back in my country.

Meanwhile, there was talk in Bombay about the establishment of a National Stock Exchange. My elder son, Sanjay, was keen to try his luck in starting a trading business because he had experience working with Merrill Lynch in New York. So he bought a trading card and we began a share trading service in Bombay. Like the housekeeping firm in Saudi Arabia, this practice was also called Alba.

Both my sons were on board and I cautioned them to trade only on behalf of people they knew. Trading was a high-risk business. "If they run away when they lose money, how will we find them?" I would reason with them. Sanjay's hunger for success pushed the business to grow quickly enough to attract the attention of Mr. Jehangir Wadia, a dynamic businessman with a sharp acumen for perceiving potential. He was an astute investor who pumped money into fledgling businesses, nurtured their growth and then sold them.

As the business starting flourishing, the Harshad Mehta scam hit the market and took everyone down.

While our family business recovered from this shock, we were hopeful of being able to start afresh with a new opportunity, together.

Right around then, the dotcom boom was about to reach its zenith and we launched Online Solutions Pvt. Ltd in 1995, which designed websites, maintained servers, developed e-portals and serviced other needs of the burgeoning industry.

For the first time, I was manufacturing a product I could not touch and feel.

I now saw a different work ethic—young men and women commuted for two hours one way and worked overnight. Mattresses were laid out wall-to-wall in one room so that the programmers could catch a quick nap when they were exhausted. The women, married with children, would juggle household duties and this demanding profession. These efforts bore fruit, and within a year, the company grew to have 60 people on its payroll. The company garnered great momentum and had mergers that now transformed our online business into a multimillion-dollar company. However, the dotcom bubble burst in March 2000 and didn't spare our business either.

By this time, my definition of success had begun to change. I started channelling my energy to philanthropy and charity, away from making money. I joined Rotary Club of Bombay Central. The motto of Rotary is 'Service before self'. I will always hold my connection with the Rotary community very close to my heart. This network of good samaritans has taught me so much about philosophy, fellowship, kindness, charity and building a community to help others.

I WAS IN POSSESSION OF SOMETHING THAT NO ONE COULD GIVE ME, OR TAKE AWAY FROM ME—PEACE AND CONTENTMENT.

As humility, unconditional charity and affection became my touchstones of success, I started seeing people differently, and even cut myself off from some 'failures'. I stopped engaging with people who hungered for more money, more business and more connections.

I had long exited the business world and knew that now people wanted to be around me for my social worth. My last name carried much weight for those who cared about such things. But I recognised that the people I considered successful liked me because I didn't want anything from them. And I was in possession of something that no one could give me, or take away from me—peace and contentment.

I recall the beautiful lessons I have learnt from my friendship with PP, who significantly impacted my life with the way he would conduct himself. P. P. Chhabria, whom I fondly called PP, would say, "I have never known happiness until I met you." He was one of the most successful men I knew, both in the materialistic and spiritual sense of the word. He was born into a wealthy family in Karachi, but they lost their fortune overnight when PP was about seven years old. They dealt in cotton and lived in a large haveli, and when things took a downturn because of a failing family business, everything was lost. PP's mother had already passed away and his brothers were too busy trying to earn money. The boy, who once had servants to put his socks on for him, would wander around aimlessly since his family could not even afford school fees. A cook, who once worked in their haveli, saw the boy in the market and asked him what he was doing there. "I live over there," the cook said pointing to a small room above a shop, after PP told him how he was trying to fend for himself. "Come every afternoon. I'll make lunch for you." And this is how PP grew up, fed by a kind person.

Soon, he was hired as a shop boy. He would open the shop and clean it up before the owner came and then run odd jobs. After Partition, PP went to Pune in Maharashtra and would sell light bulbs on a cycle.

From these humble beginnings, he built up a mammoth empire. By the time PP and I became friends, his individual net worth rose and he had two private jets. And yet, every time he sat in one of them, he would ask the pilot or stewardess, "Is this my plane? Really? Are you sure? I own a plane?" He could not believe he had achieved this.

As he got richer and older, like me, he lost his taste for materialistic pleasures. Once, both of us flew down to Goa in his plane. As we were about to get off, a member of his staff came to tell him, "Sir, the chief minister has heard you are in the state and wishes to meet you."

"Oh no!" he said. "Can you please tell him it's just a member of my company and not me who is on the plane?" The staffer obliged, but I asked him why he had refused a private meeting with such an important man. "Oh, he'll come and force an introduction with someone else who wants to meet me and then they will talk business. Then they will make plans for the evening and force me to meet others. I've come here to enjoy my time with you and have light-hearted conversations. I don't want to get caught up in all that," was his reply.

He never forgot his humble beginnings and as polite as he was to people of his social status, he was kinder and humbler to his staff and those who worked for him. He bought each of them apartments of their own and ensured they were well looked after even after he was gone.

Besides PP, many such successful men and women showed me the path to happiness, through service, including Daulat Hariani, Dilip Lakhi, Baldev Idnani, Amar Daulatani, Dilip Kapoor and Devendra Garg.

In the later years, I have become as determined to better myself as I was in my younger years to avoid it. I observed my peers closely to see what gave them peace, what made them happy and how they expanded their life beyond the gross needs of '*roti, kapda aur makaan*' to make a larger impact.

Many of my life lessons were imbibed from the 'Hospital' Hindujas; not on how to become more successful in the monetary sense, but as human beings by sharing prosperity and creating a legacy.

We are not all related by blood, but have shared a kinship due to the common last name. The Hinduja clan had lived together in a large haveli back in Shikarpur, Sindh, before the Partition. In my struggles as a youth, I am grateful to the guidance I received from Srichand Hinduja and Gopichand Hinduja, known to everyone as SP and GP respectively.

Our bond continued from Shikarpur, Sindh to Khar, Mumbai. From going to the same Khatwari Darbar temple to our parents enjoying early morning walks, I can never forget our times together and the amount of love and help SP and GP have provided me in my life as a student in Mumbai, young businessman in Saudi Arabia, philanthropist in IndusInd Foundation and good friend through music. Thanks to their international work and cultural pursuits, I have had the opportunity to interact with many business tycoons, politicians, diplomats, ambassadors, artists and singers across the world.

Looking at their generous support, I learned how one could help someone without spending money. One can be generous with one's contacts, or be warm enough to be a friend in a foreign country, or simply nurture them with home-cooked meals.

To make a change in this world, be wealthy with your conduct, not just material possessions.

SEVEN

JOURNEY BEYOND THE SELF

After setting my sons on the path to success, I became restless. I no longer had the drive to keep chasing money. My mind wandered to so many people who were seemingly rich but so unhappy that they had become self-destructive, like the world's greatest entertainer Michael Jackson. To me, an unsuccessful person is one who thinks about wealth alone and whose biggest fear is losing it.

It is not wrong to think about wealth, afterall, it has given me and my family a sense of security and peace of mind. But why can't we pursue happiness and money? With age, I started paying attention to eating right, getting proper rest and even doing some yoga. Having used my intellect to make money, investing my emotions and time to keep my family and loved ones close, I now longed to raise my spiritual quotient by doing things for the greater good, giving a purpose to my actions.

My father planted the seeds of philanthropy in me.

Since I turned 40, I had been "gifting" myself US$5,000 on my birthday each year and squirreling it away. I planned to use it for charity but hadn't zeroed down to a specific avenue for it yet. When I moved back to India, I got involved with the local Rotary club and experienced its outreach activities for the less privileged—donation of wheelchairs, eye check-up camps, cataract surgeries for senior citizens, books and stationary for students, building toilets for village schools and solar lights in hamlets.

HAVING USED MY INTELLECT TO MKE MONEY, INVESTING MY EMOTIONS AND TIME TO KEEP MY FAMILY AND LOVED ONES CLOSE, I NOW LONGED TO RAISE MY SPIRITUAL QUOTIENT BY DOING THINGS FOR THE GREATER GOOD, GIVING A PURPOSE TO MY ACTIONS.

One incident that stayed with me was how villagers near Matheran in Maharashtra wanted to install solar lights on the streets. I asked them, "Wouldn't you want the lights in your home instead? These are expensive and would be stolen".

"Our children get bitten by snakes when they walk on these roads in the dark. They don't have shoes, you see. None of us will steal these lights. Only outsiders would do that and we would immediately know who did it," explained a parent. This made me think deeply about contributing to the welfare of students and their future.

Retired from the daily grind of making money, I had enough time on hand to look at some neglected projects. One of them was the family's holiday home in Ganeshpuri, a small town close to Mumbai. The town is famous for natural hot water springs and the spiritual teachers Swami Nityanand Maharaj and Swami Muktanand Maharaj.

Years ago, my father had met Swami Nityanand and had become his disciple. Pleased with his devotion and charity, Swamiji gifted him a piece of land in Ganeshpuri. My father built a house on that land, near Ganeshpuri ashram. It is surrounded by fruit trees, vegetable patches and has a well in the garden. While my father was alive, the family would drive there for weekend getaways. We would pay our respects at the temple adjoining the springs and give alms to the needy outside the holy site.

When I was in Saudi Arabia, my wife Kanta continued this tradition, though times were hard for the family. *We may not have money to give alms*, she thought, *but by God's grace, we can still buy them vada pavs.*

However, after my father passed away, the family stopped visiting the weekend home and its upkeep was entrusted to a gardener-cum-guard.

It was several years later, in 2013, that I decided to

visit, harbouring the idea that I could turn the home into a school for underprivileged children in the area. Nityanand Maharaj loved children and I thought it would be the best way to honour both my father and his guru.

Inside, the house was in ramshackles. It would take six to eight months and over Rs 15 lakh to turn it into a place fit for children.

To find quick solutions, I met a lot of local bank officials and people from nearby communities. During one such conversation, I was introduced to Sheetal Mahale, a dynamic young teacher and dancer from Nashik. Sheetal specialises in *balwadi* (free nursery school) and immediately agreed to lead the project.

Within a week of my trip to Ganeshpuri, we performed a puja as part of the inauguration of Dream Centre, the free primary school along with Rotary members including Pammi Oberoi, Nirupama Khandolkar and Raman Abrol. We chose the name 'Dream Education Centre' because I felt every child has a dream, and this school could help them move towards it. Sheetal had gathered teachers from the nearby towns and villages; about 70 children enrolled.

The project was such a success that my Rotary group came to visit and speak to the students and their parents. "We're very happy that our children can speak in English," said more than one parent, "But now they do this *git-pit* at home and we don't understand it. We want to speak it too!" And thus started English-speaking classes for adults. My other friends wanted to contribute too. One of them noticed that the classrooms in the local municipal school which had a capacity of 60 students had only one bulb. He promptly sent his trusted electrician with the instructions to fit as many tube lights as necessary and wire them correctly.

The Dream Education Centre effect worked on the villagers too. A farmer offered about five acres of his farmland to build a proper school.

The staff and teachers of the school were so energised by the work that they asked me if they could go to other schools to teach too, after work hours at Dream Education Centre. "There are many students who can't come this far and we have the time in the afternoons," they said.

I was able to build the school with the support and leadership of dynamic women educators in Ganeshpuri including Sheetal Mahale, Pramila Kanse and Sandhya Chavan. When the school had to stay shut because of the covid-19 pandemic, Sandhya and the other teachers began reaching out to students in far off areas who had no access to technology to continue their studies.

I realised that these committed teachers were the real gems of Dream Education Centre. Together, they devised a plan to train other teachers to teach English, computers and other subjects. Dream Education Centre itself was educating 400 students, and could not take in more, but the swelling tribe of dedicated teachers were able to take this dream beyond its classroom walls to almost 15 other schools.

Meanwhile, my father's bungalow still lay vacant and decrepit. My dream was now to turn it into a college for teachers, so that the tribe grows.

Along with philanthropic responsibilities at Ganeshpuri, I was also at the helm of affairs at the IndusInd Foundation, a charitable arm of IndusInd Bank.

The bank was established in 1994 with capital contributed by businessmen from all over the world, many of whom belonged to the Sindhi community. I was one of them. Among the many charitable activities that the foundation spearheaded, the one that impacted me the most was the work being done for widows and senior citizens.

It motivated me over the years to create a happy atmosphere for women, the elderly as well as youth, everywhere I go.

The more you do, the more you feel that you are just starting.

EIGHT

LOCKDOWN MADE ME WEALTHIER

When the covid-19 pandemic took over the world in March 2020, I was in the middle of a very busy retirement. I'd go for walks every morning at Cuffe Parade, followed by yoga at home or a workout in the gym. I'd head out to my office in Fort and enjoy evening coffee from my favourite cafe followed by some leisure time at Taj Wellington Mews. My commitment to charitable institutions and Friday lunch meetings at the Rotary Club at Trident kept me inspired throughout the week.

And I wouldn't dare to refuse a movie and dinner date with Kanta twice a week.

When Mumbai went into lockdown, I expected my movements to be curtailed for a week. But as the week turned to two weeks and then a month, I began getting restless. I felt like I had fallen asleep in one world and woken up in another. All the activities stopped, and the only thing that visited me now was gloom—the number of people stolen by the disease, the falling stocks, the crumbling economy, the misery of the poor making their way back to their home towns.

For weeks, I could not get myself to do anything productive. Slowly, as the lockdown became the new normal, I saw how much better off I was than most. Though we had to trim our domestic staff, there were still those who lived with Kanta and me, so we were spared the tiring daily chores. Food was scarce outside the city for some days, but our kitchen was well-stocked, thanks to Kanta's efficiency and planning. There was no access to money for a few weeks, but Kanta had saved up enough cash for our daily needs. Our home became our refuge—the searing summer could not touch us, nor could cyclone Nisarga. Fresh air was aplenty, and medical assistance was only a phone call away. My family was safe and close at hand, a mere few kilometres away. But hugs and kisses from my grandchildren suddenly posed a threat. They refrained from visiting us as an act of love as Kanta and I were immuno-compromised.

FOR WEEKS, I COULD NOT GET MYSELF TO DO ANYTHING PRODUCTIVE. SLOWLY, AS THE LOCKDOWN BECAME THE NEW NORMAL, I SAW HOW MUCH BETTER OFF I WAS THAN MOST.

Days seemed like a never ending loop—I was living the

same 24 hours repeatedly as the lockdown extended every week. Respite came in the form of poet and lyricist Gulzar. His verses posted on social media seemed like he spoke for everyone when he said, "*Yeh waqt bhi kitna ajeeb hai/ Pehle milta nahin tha/ ab guzarta nahin hai.*" (Time is such a strange creature/ We couldn't find enough of it earlier/ Now it doesn't seem to pass).

Slowly, like people all over the world, I realised how disposable the trappings of life were. We could survive without luxury cars, take-outs from fancy restaurants, bespoke fashion and limited edition watches. What I missed most was the company of my friends and loved ones, especially my office staff and the people I met at the club in the evenings. As Gulzar said, '*Sochta hu ki dosto par/ mukadma kar du/ issi bahane tareekh par/mulakaat hoti rahegi*' (I am thinking of suing my friends/ This way at least/ I will get to meet them at court proceedings).

GP came down from London, but his busy schedule kept us from planning a relaxed catch-up.

"Why don't we set up a group video call one of these days," I suggested to him one day. "Then you can speak to everyone who wants to meet you." Group video calls had become the new normal of lockdown life. Schools used it to conduct classes for students; companies used it for meetings with all the employees sitting at home in different cities and even countries; friends used it to catch up; doctors used it for consultations; professionals used it to conduct 'webinars' to upgrade their skills. Even birthday parties were being conducted through group video calls.

"Good idea," said GP, "Why don't you set it up and tell everyone." So, with my son's help, I set up the first Zoom call for about six to eight participants. Everyone thought this was a great idea and was excited to attend.

The first session had many glitches as industrialists, leaders of business empires, religious leaders and global philanthropists tried to navigate technology independently. Most of them had a grandchild sitting next to them for tech support!

One session was not enough. There were more people—friends, relatives and those who wanted to maintain their social ties with my influential cousin. I realised that the rich don't have friends or relatives. They have courtiers.

Within a week, the Zoom call became a regular morning ritual, attended by over 15 people. First GP sang the song '*Ae malik tere bande hum*' by his favourite playback singers Lata Mangeshkar and Vasant Desai. Then followed classical and non-classical singers who enthralled the attendees with bhajans, thumris and all kinds of songs, stopping to explain what the words meant or share a story behind the composition. Padma Bhushan awardee singer Anup

Jalota would wear a new kurta daily for the call and gave the simplest relationship advice in a humorous way. Pankaj Udhas' cousin, Pradeep Udhas, also has a melodious voice quite like Talat Mahmood's. He'd sing some soft, romantic songs. One evening, playback singer Sonu Nigam joined us on the call and livened up the gathering of nearly 450 people with his hit songs.

I saw that the global pandemic was a great equaliser and connected artists and creative people with their fans directly. With no song recordings, concerts, tours, or adoring mobs, singers were shorn of their celebrity status and reduced to their essence—pure talent and love for the craft. All they needed was an appreciative audience.

I SAW THAT THE GLOBAL PANDEMIC WAS A GREAT EQUALISER AND CONNECTED ARTISTS AND CREATIVE PEOPLE WITH THEIR FANS DIRECTLY.

Soon, a diverse variety of people joined our Zoom calls. We had a new morning ritual— 8.30 to 10 in the mornings became the most intellectually stimulating time for me. Spiritual leaders who lived in ashrams in the Himalayas reported how clean the Ganga had become since the world went into lockdown. A fourth-generation Ayurveda doctor in Rishikesh said elephants had been spotted coming to drink from the holy river. A person in charge of the Ayodhya

Trust read out his poetry. Business tycoons debated topics such as 'What is more powerful—time or money?' or 'desire versus happiness' and whether light and darkness can go hand-in-hand. Another spiritual leader talked about the ancient wisdom embedded in Hinduism. Someone close to the Nehru family revealed how the Constitution of India was written in his family home.

Other luminaries of this Zoom conference included a film distributor and producer responsible for taking 70 per cent of all Indian movies released in a year to cinema halls abroad.

Another man called himself singer-actor-director Kishore Kumar's 'superfan'. Not only did he know and sing all the songs of the playback singer, he had also gone to his birthplace, Khandwa in Madhya Pradesh, and shot a video of himself singing there.

A successful jeweller from Dubai, whose clients included Arab royalty, took a keen interest in the Vedic etymology of names. He had a deep knowledge of the subject, and everyone in the group sent him their names to discover their meaning, history and mystical connection.

Mesmerised by such august company, I learned to keep my mouth shut and listen. I noticed that whatever the topic was, people started by talking about themselves and their life experiences and only spoke about the matter at hand for 30 seconds. No matter the success and recognition they had garnered, they needed to feel seen. There was so much to see, hear, learn and experience just by sitting in front of a screen.

Slowly, all my activities shifted online. The yoga teacher conducted Zoom sessions and I signed up for one every day to maintain my health. Things also changed around me. A bigshot restaurateur had been my neighbour for years, and I had seen him hurrying out on numerous mornings, ear-to-phone, ducking into his large car, brows furrowed. But now, he suddenly stopped to greet me every time we crossed paths. "Hello, sir. How are you? Everything okay at home?" he would ask. *What happened to him?* I wondered, and immediately got the reply, *What happened to you? The same thing happened to him!*

Covid-19 had taught what no school, religion or college had been able to impart so far—the importance of connecting to another human being. One is not happy because of what one has, but because of who one is.

After a month or so, the world saw the Earth heal—the skies were clearer and bluer and new birdsongs were heard in the absence of traffic. Gharials, dolphins and other aquatic life were visible after decades, and migratory birds flocked in numbers more prominent than before. The planet showed that it did not need humans to thrive; humans needed the planet. They were trapped in the cages that were their homes while all the animals were free.

On the home front, after the initial irritation of being cooped up, I learnt the value of controlling my mind and my tongue. "Is it necessary to say this? Will I get anything out of it?" I would ask myself before saying anything.

I would graciously let minor irritations pass and solaced Kanta by even using the guest bathroom to give her space. "I'm just going to let the taps run in that one," I would say, "We don't want them to rust out of disuse." With no outside staff, my tantrums about how I'd like things done were gone.

Left only with each other, we became playful. "How much do you pay for a haircut?" asked Kanta when I requested one. "About a thousand rupees," I said. "Well, I'll charge ten thousand rupees," she replied, knowing well that I had no cash on me.

In the evenings, I would sing songs with coarse lyrics that made my teenage grandchildren roll their eyes. I would gesture, taking something out of my head and dumping it out of the window. "What are you doing?" my grandchildren would ask. "Taking the *kachra* out of my head and throwing it. I want a clean mind," I'd reply. "Dada is going senile," they would say and retreat to their rooms.

IF WE CONCENTRATE ON OUR BLESSINGS, EVEN A PANDEMIC CAN BECOME A RICH PLACE FOR THE HAPPY SOUL.

When the lockdown eased in the first weeks of June 2020, our son Sanjay took Kanta and me for a spin in South Mumbai. It had been almost three months since we last stepped out. Mumbai, the city that never sleeps, seemed comatose—all the shops on the bustling Colaba Causeway were shut; there were no walkers or joggers on Marine Drive; the city's business area, Nariman Point, seemed like a ghost town; no lawyers were crossing the road at Fort to get to the High Court. Even the iconic art galleries of Kala Ghoda were bereft of enthusiasts. The iron and steel skeletons of the metro work were standing, but drills and cranes no longer snarled and rumbled around them.

I realised that time is like a glass of water–it changes colour according to what we put in it. It is half full if we have peace and satisfaction, but half empty if we are troubled by desire. If we concentrate on our blessings, even a pandemic can become a rich place for the happy soul.

The choice to be happy is within you.

NINE

WORLD'S BEST RELIGION

In retirement, I have no time to "network" with successful people talking about stocks and shares only to see how each person can benefit from me materially. But I have all the time for boyish pursuits and my partner in these is Jangoo Motafram from the Parsi colony in Colaba, Cusrow Baug.

Jangoo has a unique talent for knowing where the best food, at subsidised rates, is available in the city's financial district—Fort, Flora Fountain and Nariman Point. Both of us relish a scrumptious thali at the Standard Chartered employee canteen for a mere Rs 30, or snacks at the employee canteens at Central Bank or Union Bank. Jangoo also has a nose for Annual General Meetings of large public quoted firms such as Reliance and Tata. I love his investigative enthusiasm with which he often shares, "The Reliance meeting will just have tea and biscuits. But the Tata one is being held at the Taj hotel so there will be cakes and sandwiches and all the frills of high tea. Let's go there."

Jangoo is also a music lover like me. So every few days, he comes over with a newspaper cutting of a live musical show happening close by we could go to. He does not have much to give but is happy to part with whatever he has.

I once had a harmonium in my house. When it lay unused for many years, I gave it away to Dream Education Centre in Ganeshpuri, thinking it would be of better service to the teachers and students there. Then when the imposed lockdown during the pandemic revived my interest in music, I wished I had my old harmonium. I mentioned this to Jangoo, and he quickly responded, "I have a 30-year-old harmonium lying around if you want it. You'll have to repair it, though." I jumped at the offer. It amused me to repair an old instrument instead of buying a new one. It was an adventure to find someone to repair such an antique specimen, but I found one and got it ready for Rs 5,000. I knew maintenance would require regular time, effort and finances, but I didn't mind. I appreciated having something with character that I could cherish. When I took to singing at competitions held at Rotary Club, Jangoo found me a tutor—Viraf Daruwalla—to guide me.

I APPRECIATED HAVING SOMETHING WITH CHARACTER THAT I COULD CHERISH.

For all my eccentricities, I saw God in Jangoo. His simple boyish adventures, disinterest in my wealth and position, and lack of airs and grace reminded me of the simple friendships I had enjoyed in Chembur's refugee camp when my family came to India during the Partition.

I honour this friendship by inviting Jangoo to our family's Diwali puja every year. It is a celebration meant only for family members and Jangoo is family to me.

I am a man of many friends, but the ones I consider closest are those I am bound to by food, music and *masti*–those who have no affectations of success, wealth and stature.

Music is a religion that doesn't divide people based on caste, looks or wealth, in my opinion. Only the voice and whether you sing from the heart matters. I have also noticed that choice of songs reveals the person's essence. Romantic and sensitive people choose soft, sonorous numbers. Pessimists are drawn to mournful ballads. Playful optimists belt out joyous songs. And the mature intellectual knows that every mood has its theme and melody, giving equal respect to them.

Through my weekly meetings at the Rotary Club, I met two music aficionados—Tejasa Zaveri and Ramnath Khanduja. Tejasa had sung a song at the beginning of a Rotary programme and as soon as it was over, I went up to her to say, "*Tum to Lata Mangeshkar ho*!" (You are Lata Mangeshkar!).

I have been a bathroom singer most of my life. But, this young friend, Tejasa Zaveri nudged me to sing on stage for the first time.

I ENCOURAGED HER TO START A SINGING GROUP FOR THE ROTARY MEMBERS; SHE TOOK UP THE PROJECT ENTHUSIASTICALLY, GENTLY COAXING OUT THE NIGHTINGALES HIDDEN IN SHY HOMEMAKERS AND SERIOUS BUSINESS PEOPLE.

I encouraged her to start a singing group for the Rotary members; she took up the project enthusiastically, gently coaxing out the nightingales hidden in shy homemakers and serious business people. She knew I loved to sing and suggested I perform at an important function held with all the Rotary clubs of Mumbai. "Okay, put down my name," I said enthusiastically, "All I have to do is put the noose around my neck, right? I'll do that." I thought I would croak a few lines from movie songs by playback singers Mukesh , Kishore Kumar and Hemant Kumar and get back to my seat.

But Tejasa would not let me go so quickly. She began to coach me every day, and if I didn't practise, she would call up my wife to ensure I did.

Her sincere, loving nature won me over; after seeing how much effort she was putting in to ensure I sang well, I doubled my efforts.

I started classes with Indian music teacher Viraf Daruwalla and practised diligently. Viraf taught me that my voice was more suited to low-pitch songs like those sung by Hemant Kumar, Jagjit Singh and Kishore Kumar. He also taught me to play with each word to bring life to the music.

Singing slowly became a part of my daily life, enriching the lockdown period during the covid-19 pandemic throughout 2020, 2021 and early 2022. I discovered apps such as StarMaker, where I could partner with someone sitting across the globe and stitch our parts into a duet. The family indulged my newfound passion; my sister, Maya Rajani, gifted me a karaoke machine for Rakshabandhan, much to my delight. Now, I had a professional microphone to practise with high-quality background music and sound engineering for my daily sessions.

Towards the beginning of 2021, I also began making videos for my songs, taking great delight in figuring out the look and feel of the video and deciding what I would wear . "On the inside, I am a director," I thought, taking inspiration from my professional singer friends. I would go to Ameya Naik (who runs a studio in Malabar Hill) with my ideas, and we would shoot it together. I then launched them on my YouTube channel, beginning with a tribute to ghazal maestro Jagjit Singh. I sang the hit '*Hothon se chhoo lo tum*' and shared it with my friends who were delighted. GP called me from London to say, "Arre! You are such a talented fellow." Feeling encouraged, I lined up about 50 more songs and began visualising how they would be shot for my YouTube channel. Today, my YouTube channel is my online oasis of happiness to make and share memories while singing.

This YouTube channel 'Gul Sings For You' is now part of my legacy where I celebrate loving friendships with old and new while singing and making the world sing with us.

Religion brings people together from diverse backgrounds and cultures. That is why, music is above all religions.

TEN

BUILD A LIFE OF EXPERIENCES, NOT EXPECTATIONS

Each day begins with hopes and ends with dreams. Leave behind the passive dreaming of a rose-tinted future. The energy of happiness exists in living today with roots sunk firmly in reality's soil.

My life's story is a collection of numerous experiences that made me richer as a human being. No money and worldly material possessions can match this. The richness I feel deep within my bones today lies in the kindness, wisdom, friendships, support and love I have received through all the highs and lows of this long, fulfilling journey I have taken.

EACH DAY BEGINS WITH HOPES AND ENDS WITH DREAMS.

Was it easy? By no means. On the surface what looked like multiple failures to the world, in fact helped me develop genuine character and the ability to stay true to who I am, continue to learn with all my might and stay young at heart. Youthfulness is not determined by age but by our attitude

SUCCESS AND FAILURE ARE JUST WORDS— DON'T LET THEM DEFINE YOUR LIFE.

and hope. There were challenges but I advanced continually and that is the biggest message I want you, my readers, to remember from my story.

Even if things don't unfold the way you expected, don't be disheartened or give up. Success and failure are just words–don't let them define your life. A person's true nature is revealed during adversity. The institutions of human society treat us as parts of a machine. They assign us ranks and place considerable pressure on us to fulfill defined roles. We need something to help us restore humanity. Choose art and culture as your messengers of peace and hope, just as I used this book to give voice to the feelings that have built up inside me over so many years.

Spread love and kindness through your work, in your families and among friends. Behaviour is always greater than knowledge. In life, there are many situations where knowledge fails but behaviour can handle everything. Study well, work smart, save money and enjoy to your heart's content. But let go of ego. Life is a celebration. There will be speed breakers and bumps, but nothing is constant. Don't be so serious.

SPREAD LOVE AND KINDNESS THROUGH YOUR WORK, IN YOUR FAMILIES AND AMONG FRIENDS.

STUDY WELL, WORK SMART, SAVE MONEY AND ENJOY TO YOUR HEART'S CONTENT. BUT LET GO OF EGO.

Just flow and keep your heart open to opportunities. Allow life to surprise you in ways you may never have imagined. Be childlike, it will always help you find creative solutions to life's unique challenges and circumstances.

For instance, I never saved money for myself but only for my wife. In our family of four, we were able to weather so many struggles only because of Kanta's habit of saving money consistently. She collected all the coins I gave her besides my earnings. She opened fixed deposits and invested in the stock market, and this money accumulated and multiplied in many ways. Her creative ways of saving money in small instalments over a period of time helped us not just sail through difficult financial times but also build a healthy relationship with money. We started valuing what we had and became conscious of how we saved, spent and created wealth—not just for ourselves but for people and communities in need.

The biggest gift you can give the world is your generosity and the awareness of its impact. It needs a firm resolve to spare your time and resources with the world. Many people are in the position to help but they don't because of the insecurity of losing what they have or just being indifferent.

True generosity lies in what you give through your actions and not what you broadcast to the world with well-packaged words in today's social media-driven era.

I hope reading my book encourages you to reflect and expand, and enrich your personality with love, kindness, patience and laughter.